The World is your Oyster

AR Knight

Acknowledgments

This book would not have come to fruition had it not been for a monumental effort by my wife, Lisa. She provided me with the courage to dream of getting a book published and then the energy and expertise to see it through.

The images you see in this book represent many hours spent in the water by some dedicated photographers. I share their love of the ocean but, unfortunately, not their photographic skills.

To Bruce Kennedy, my agent, and to Fiona Schultz at New Holland, thank you for your belief in the book and your patience with someone new to the game.

Foreword

You will find some truly incredible images in this book. Images of small, frightened fish, a dolphin leaping for joy and even two manatee seemingly holding hands, sharing a romantic moment. These images, combined with the text, help to draw parallels between our lives and the lives of all marine creatures. *The World is your Oyster* shows that even though we don't have scales or dorsal fins our lives are not that dissimilar. We all know love, fear, sadness and joy.

For those of you who have had the opportunity to view and marvel at coral reefs and underwater wonderlands, I hope this book helps to keep your memories alive. For those of you who haven't paid a visit, I hope it inspires you to do so.

Yes, the world is our oyster, as the cliché goes, and that makes us magnificent pearls. But remember, we are nothing without the oyster—protect, nurture and love it for the generations to come.

Ashley Knight

A world of brilliant blooms

and colourful characters.

A magical place

where you are one of a kind

and there's a world of
adventure and discoveries
awaiting you each and every day.

Things that will make you laugh,

things that will amaze you

and even scare you.

There's disco dancing—
John Travolta style,

outrageous outfits

and warm, soothing baths
after a long, hard day.

There are friends to meet,

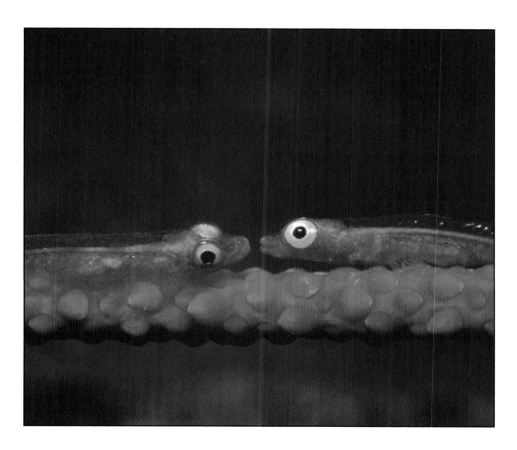

to share your
deepest secrets with,

and your best jokes.

There are special friends too
(the romantic kind).

You start with some dancing,
to get you in the mood,

and before you know it
you are holding hands,

and snuggling,

and kissing—long, sloppy kisses,

and then...

you discover that size
doesn't really matter.

But you know the most awesome thing about your world— it's a place where dreams come true. The sky is not the limit.

Show your true colours,

spread your wings

and fly.

Why, you could be a star
if you want to be,

or if you've got big lips,
maybe a famous singer,

or you could be the best
mum in the whole world.

You could be a clown and run away to join the circus,

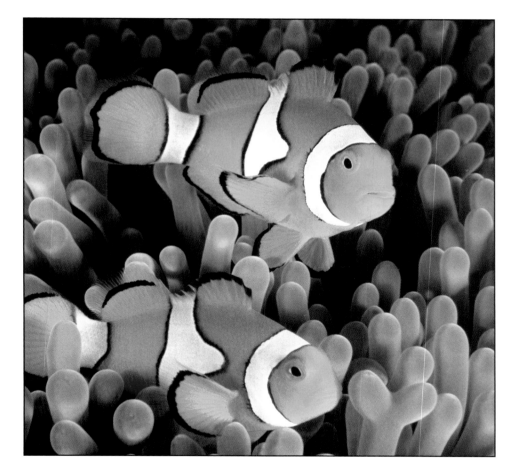

or simply be a great friend.

It's your choice,
after all, it's your oyster.

The long and the short
of it is though,

there may be obstacles on
the path to your dreams.

Big obstacles,
and seeing beyond them
can seem impossible.

This makes your world
appear more like a maze
than an oyster,

and as for your dreams, well,
they just look so far away!

This can make you feel flat,

and off colour

and you feel like pulling
inside your shell and giving up.

But remember, there is always light at the end of the tunnel

and anything is possible
if you put your mind to it.

Just don't be afraid
to stick your neck out,

to get out of your
comfort zone,

to take a big, deep breath

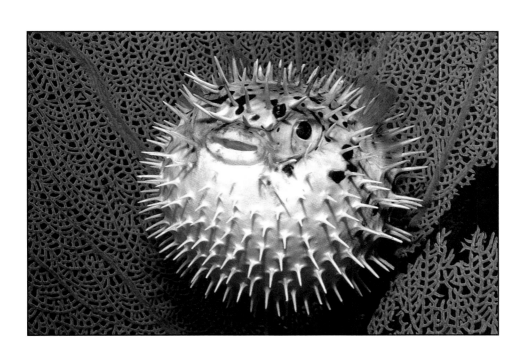

and step into the unknown.

Because you never know
what treasures await you there.

First published in Australia in 2004 by
New Holland Publishers (Australia) Pty Ltd
Sydney • Auckland • London • Cape Town

14 Aquatic Drive Frenchs Forest NSW 2086 Australia
218 Lake Road Northcote Auckland New Zealand
86 Edgware Road London W2 2EA United Kingdom
80 McKenzie Street Cape Town 8001 South Africa

A record of the Cataloguing-in-Publication Data for this book is available from
the National Library of Australia.

Managing Editor: Monica Berton
Project Editor: Liz Hardy
Designer: Joanne Buckley
Production Manager: Linda Bottari
Printer: Times Offset, Malaysia

10 9 8 7 6 5 4 3 2 1

Photographs courtesy of:
Great Barrier Reef Marine Park Authority pages 5, 23, 25, 43, 47, 55, 69; **Marine Themes**
pages 13, 15, 17, 27, 29, 35, 45, 53, 59, 63, 67, 71, 87; **Gary Bell/oceanwideimages.com**
pages 7, 9, 11,19, 39, 57, 61, 75, 81, 83, 89; **Australian Picture Library** pages 21, 33, 49, 51,
73, 77, 79, 93; **Jason Jennings and Lisa Knight** pages 65, 95; **Auscape International** pages
41, 85; **Photolibrary** pages 31, 37; **Getty Images** page 91.
Cover image courtesy of **Marine Themes**